Name _____

Front Row Seat

Grandma and Grandpa fly in from Florida. Aunt Marta and Uncle Pablo drive down from Oregon. Mom and Dad buy six extra tickets for Maria's very best friends. Maria peeks around the curtain and sees a roomful of shiny, proud faces. And there, right in the front row, sit all of her relatives and friends! They want to see her dance.

Check.

This story is about how Maria's friends and relatives...

☐ want to see her dance. ☐ fly in from Florida.

Match.

Grandma and Grandpa   buy six extra tickets.

Mom and Dad   drive down from Oregon.

Aunt Marta and Uncle Pablo   fly in from Florida.

Write.

What does Maria see when she peeks around the curtain?

_____

- -

_____

Circle.

Maria's friends and relatives are sitting in the...

last row.   third row.   front row.

• Draw a picture of yourself in the front row.

Marry Me, Beth!

At recess time, the kids wait for Beth by the door. They all want her to be their friend. If the girls play "Marry Me," the boys don't get mad if Beth catches them. They don't seem to run so fast. If the class plays dodgeball, Beth is the first one picked. Beth is nice to everyone, and everyone is nice to her.

Check.

This story is about a girl who
☐ wants friends.
☐ everyone likes.

Circle yes or no.

How do you know that everyone likes Beth?

Beth is the last one picked for dodgeball.	Yes	No
Kids wait for her by the door at recess.	Yes	No
The boys don't get mad if she catches them.	Yes	No
She is the first one picked for dodgeball.	Yes	No
Everyone is mean to her.	Yes	No

Circle and color.

When Beth catches them in "Marry Me," the boys are...

Shortcut

After the school play, on a dark, dark night, the gang walks by a dark, dark lot. Jack wants to take a shortcut and asks, "Who will go in first?" No one says a word. Everyone knows that ghosts play there. Cassie says, "I'll be brave and go in first." She runs quickly through the lot. Then she yells, "Okay, Jack. Now it's your turn." Jack does not want to go!

Check.

What is the main idea of this story?

☐ The gang walks by a dark lot.

☐ Jack changes his mind about the shortcut.

Write.

_____ runs quickly through the lot.

_____ asks, "Who will go in first?"

_____ does not want to go!

_____ says, "I'll be brave and go in first."

Write.

Why doesn't anyone want to go in the dark, dark lot?

_____

_____

• Draw a picture of something you did to show you were brave.

If Cassie Was Invisible

If Cassie was invisible, she would go to school and not do any work because her teacher couldn't see her. She would stay up late and go to bed in her jeans and t-shirt. Then, she stops and thinks. If she was invisible, she wouldn't get any apple pie and ice cream. And no one would ask her to play if they couldn't see her. Maybe being invisible wouldn't be so much fun after all.

Underline.

This story is about what Cassie would do...

        if no one asked her to play

        if she was invisible.

Circle yes or no.

If Cassie was invisible, she would . . .

stay up late.	Yes No
get apple pie and ice cream.	Yes No
go to bed in her jeans and T-shirt.	Yes No
be asked to play.	Yes No
go to school and not do any work.	Yes No

Write.

What does Cassie think about being invisible at the end of the story?

_____

– –

_____

•SOMETHING EXTRA•

Draw a picture of what you would do if you were invisible.

What Does It Say?

When it's time to go home from school, Miss Freed gives Donald a note for his mom and dad. Donald wonders about what it says. Did Miss Freed see me stick out my tongue in spelling? Did she see me cut in line for a drink of water? Did she see me draw that funny picture of the new girl and pass it around in reading? Donald says to himself, "I'll be really good tomorrow!"

Check.

What is the main idea of this story?

☐ Donald wonders what the note says.

☐ Donald cuts in line for a drink.

Circle yes or no.

Donald wonders if Miss Freed saw him...

stick his tongue out.	Yes No
throw his lunch away.	Yes No
cut in line.	Yes No
pass a note.	Yes No

Can Dudley come to school next Tuesday and cook a Chinese dinner for our class?

Thank you,
Miss Freed

Check.

Read Donald's note.

Miss Freed wants   ☐ Dudley
☐ Mom and Dad

to cook a Chinese dinner for her   ☐ mother   next   ☐ Monday.
☐ class   ☐ Tuesday.

Story Without Words

First Position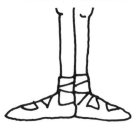

Second Position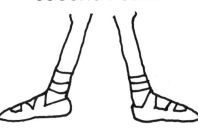

Tonight, Maria will dance in the story called "Sleeping Beauty." She will help tell the story without talking or singing. Dancing that tells a story without words is called "ballet." Maria has been taking ballet lessons since she was six. She has learned special ways of moving her feet in ballet that are called "positions."

Third Position

Fourth Position

Check.

Tonight, Maria will dance in the story called

 "Cinderella."

 "Sleeping Beauty."

Circle.

She will help tell the story without...

talking or singing.

dancing or smiling.

Check.

Dancing that tells a story without words

is called ☐ tap dancing.

☐ ballet.

Color the ballet shoes.

First Position – red

Second Position – blue

Third Position – green

Fourth Position – yellow

Excuse Me!

Cassie and Jackie go to the movies on Saturday afternoon. They will see a movie and three cartoons for only two dollars each. Cassie stands in line to buy popcorn and soft drinks. Jackie finds two good seats for them in the second row. The lights go off, and the movie starts. Cassie is trying to find her seat. "Oops! Excuse me!" It's very hard to find your seat when it's dark at the movies on Saturday afternoon.

Write.

Where do Cassie and Jackie go on Saturday afternoon?

_____

– – – – – – – – – – – – – – – – – – – –

_____

Underline.

Cassie stands in line to buy   candy   and   soft drinks.
                               popcorn   milk.

Check.

Jackie finds two good seats for them in the ☐ third   row.
                                            ☐ second

Write.

What does Cassie say when she can't find her seat?

_____

– – – – – – – – – – – – – – – – – – – –

_____

Cannonball Contest

Cassie, Kim and Beth are having a cannonball contest. You will be the judge! The girls go to the deep end of the pool. They all stand on the same line and wait until the coast is clear. Then, they run their fastest and jump high into the air. They grab their knees and put their heads down low. Splash! Which girl wins the contest?

Circle.

Cassie, Kim and Beth are having a   diving   contest.
                                      cannonball

Write.

Who is the judge of the contest?

_____

- -

_____

Check.

They wait until ☐ the coast is clear   and run their ☐ slowest.
                ☐ people are in the pool   ☐ fastest.

Circle.

They grab their   ears   and put their   heads   down low.
                   knees   arms

•SOMETHING EXTRA•
Color the best cannonball red.

Midnight

Kim has a horse with a spot on her nose and a long, fluffy tail. Kim calls her Midnight because of the time she was born. Her color is tan (yellow and brown). Midnight is called a filly because she's a girl and younger than four. Midnight likes to eat hay and small pieces of candy. She can run fast and jump over fences.

Write.

| nose   legs   tail |

Midnight has a spot on her _____

and a long, fluffy _____.

Circle.

Kim calls her Midnight because of   her color.

the time she was born.

Check.

I'm called a filly because I'm...

☐ a boy.

☐ younger than four.

☐ a girl.

☐ older than four.

• Color Midnight tan.

Wanted!

Kim reads the wanted poster about One-Eyed Harry who robbed the bank last night. Harry has two mean and beady eyes. He wears a patch over one eye just to scare people. He's short, about five feet tall, and wears a polka-dot bandanna. He has a dirty beard and a long, pointed nose with a wart or two on the end. No one has gotten close enough to count them. He wears an earring in one ear, and he has one front tooth missing.

Write.

Why does One-Eyed Harry wear a patch over one eye?

_____

- -

_____

Circle yes or no.

wears a polka-dot bandanna.	Yes	No
has two kind eyes.	Yes	No
has a long, pointed nose.	Yes	No
wears an earring in his nose.	Yes	No
has one front tooth missing.	Yes	No

Check.

How tall is One-Eyed Harry?

☐ about five feet ☐ about six feet ☐ about three feet

• Draw two warts on Harry's nose.

Lemonade for Sale

Jack and Lee start a business selling lemonade. First, they make a stand from Lee's picnic table. Second, they go to the store to buy a box of lemons and a sack of sugar. Third, they squeeze the lemons and pick out the seeds. Fourth, they mix the lemon juice with sugar and cold water. Would you like to buy a cold glass of lemonade from them? It's only fifteen cents.

Circle.

Jack and Lee start a
show
business
selling
lemonade.
hot dogs.

Write in 1, 2, 3, 4 order.

go to the store to buy lemons and sugar. ☐

make a stand from Lee's picnic table. ☐

mix the lemon juice with sugar and water. ☐

squeeze the lemons and pick out the seeds. ☐

Check.

You can buy a cold glass of lemonade for
☐ fifteen cents.
☐ ten cents.

•SOMETHING EXTRA•

Make a list of things kids can sell.

Don't Dally!

Beth's Mom sends her to the store to buy bread, butter and milk. Mom tells her not to dally. On her way to the store, Beth sees a fire engine parked along the street, but she doesn't dally. Then, she sees an organ grinder. Beth keeps on walking. Next, she meets some friends who ask her to play ball. She doesn't dally and walks into the store. Now, she can't remember what to buy!

Check.

Beth's Mom sends her to the store to buy...

☐ an organ grinder.   ☐ bread, butter and milk.

Write in 1, 2, 3 order.

meets some friends who ask her to play ball. ☐

sees a fire engine parked along the street. ☐

sees an organ grinder. ☐

Circle.

"Dally" means to   take too much time to do something.

do something in a hurry.

Color.

Help Beth remember what to buy. Draw a picture of bread, butter and milk.

Dudley Goes to School

Donald takes Dudley to a special school for dogs. Yesterday, Dudley learned how to do those usual dog things like how to sit, fetch and come. Today, he learns how to drive a car. Tomorrow, he will learn how to cook a Chinese dinner. Dudley is a very smart dog. He is at the top of his class. Do you know a dog that can drive a car or cook a Chinese dinner?

Write.

Where does Donald take Dudley?

_____

- -

_____

Write.

yesterday	today	tomorrow

Check.

Dudley is at the ☐ bottom
☐ top   of his class.

•SOMETHING EXTRA•

Draw a picture of something special you would like to teach Dudley to do.

Dudley's Portrait

Donald likes to paint portraits of people and animals. He feels lucky because he can draw and paint well. First, he draws Dudley's portrait with a pencil. Second, he erases and makes the changes he wants. Third, he colors Dudley's portrait with paints. Dudley is curious to see how his portrait will look.

Check.

Donald likes to paint portraits of ☐ houses ☐ people and ☐ animals. ☐ trees.

Unscramble and write.

A word for a picture of a person or animal is _____.

tproiatr

Write in 1, 2, 3 order.

Circle.

Dudley is surprised / curious to see how his portrait will look.

•SOMETHING EXTRA•
Draw a portrait of a friend or pet. Follow Donald's steps. Use your crayons.

Not Now, Dudley!

Donald and Lee are playing with trucks. Dudley feels left out. He brings them his ball, wagging his tail. "Not now, Dudley," say Donald and Lee. Dudley is sad and hurt. So he gets a stick, a good one to fetch, and gives them his best sad dog look. Donald and Lee know that dogs have feelings too. "Now, Dudley!" they say.

Circle.

When Donald and Lee are playing with trucks, Dudley feels...

surprised.   happy.   left out.

Check.

Dudley feels sad and hurt because Donald and Lee say,

☐ "Now, Dudley!"

☐ "Not now, Dudley!"

Write.

Dudley gets a _____
                    bone, stick

and gives them his best _____ dog look.
                          sad, happy

Check.

Donald and Lee know that dogs have ☐ feelings. ☐ trucks.

•SOMETHING EXTRA•

Draw a picture of something you did when you felt left out.

Company

All of Lee's relatives are coming for dinner tonight. Lee is not very happy. He'll have to be nice, like sugar and spice, and wear that suit Grandma gave him. When they pat him on the head and ask, "How is school?" he will smile and say that it's fine. He will sit on the couch and pretend not to be bored when they talk about Aunt Martha's bad back.

Check.

Lee is ☐ happy

☐ unhappy   because his relatives are coming for dinner.

Circle.

He will have to be nice like

sugar and spice.

snails and puppy dog tails.

Check.

When his relatives ask about school, Lee will...

☐ frown and say that it's awful.

☐ smile and say that it's terrible.

☐ smile and say that it's fine.

Write.

Another word for bored is not _____.

mad, interested

What will he pretend to do when they talk about Aunt Martha's bad back?

_____

_____

Beth's Spelling Test

Beth was unhappy with her spelling test. She felt let-down, or disappointed, because she missed so many words. For her next test, she worked very hard to learn her new words. She didn't miss any this time. When Beth is pleased with herself and what she has done, she feels proud.

Check.

Beth was unhappy with her …

☐ math test.   ☐ spelling test.   ☐ reading test.

Write.

Another word for let-down is _____.

disappointed, pleased

Check.

What did Beth do for her next spelling test?

☐ Beth studied her sentences.

☐ Beth studied her spelling words.

☐ Beth studied her math facts.

Circle.

When Beth is pleased with herself and what she has done, she feels…

disappointed.   lucky.   proud.

Write.

Number the pictures in 1, 2, 3 order.

Draw a happy face on the test that Beth feels proud of.

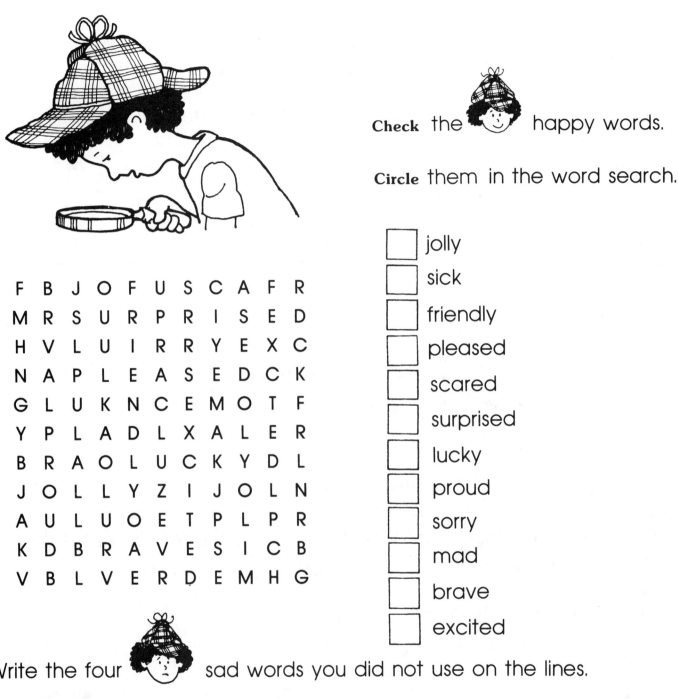

Check the 😊 happy words.

Circle them in the word search.

```
F  B  J  O  F  U  S  C  A  F  R
M  R  S  U  R  P  R  I  S  E  D
H  V  L  U  I  R  R  Y  E  X  C
N  A  P  L  E  A  S  E  D  C  K
G  L  U  K  N  C  E  M  O  T  F
Y  P  L  A  D  L  X  A  L  E  R
B  R  A  O  L  U  C  K  Y  D  L
J  O  L  L  Y  Z  I  J  O  L  N
A  U  L  U  O  E  T  P  L  P  R
K  D  B  R  A  V  E  S  I  C  B
V  B  L  V  E  R  D  E  M  H  G
```

☐ jolly
☐ sick
☐ friendly
☐ pleased
☐ scared
☐ surprised
☐ lucky
☐ proud
☐ sorry
☐ mad
☐ brave
☐ excited

Write the four 😟 sad words you did not use on the lines.

_____

Draw an orange ☐ around the word that tells how you feel when you hear a loud noise.

Draw a blue ☐ around the word that tells how you feel when someone takes a ball away from you.

Read and finish the sentences. Draw faces to show how Jack feels.

shy   worried   silly   brave   happy

1. Jack helps an old woman cross a busy
   street. _____

   _ _ _ _ _ _ _ _ _ _ _ _ _ _ _ _ _

   He feels _____.

2. Jack did not study last night. Today, he
   has a math test. _____

   _ _ _ _ _ _ _ _ _ _ _ _ _ _ _ _ _

   Jack feels _____.

3. On Halloween, he dresses up like a big
   hamburger. _____

   _ _ _ _ _ _ _ _ _ _ _ _ _ _ _ _ _

   He feels _____.

4. Tonight is his first baseball practice at his
   new school. He doesn't know anyone. _____

   _ _ _ _ _ _ _ _ _ _ _ _ _ _ _ _ _

   Jack feels _____.

5. Jack got a new bicycle for his birthday.
   _____

   _ _ _ _ _ _ _ _ _ _ _ _ _ _ _ _ _

   He feels _____.

Lacy Patterns

Kim likes to look at the lacy patterns of snowflakes with her magnifying glass. Most of them have six sides or six points. But she has never seen two snowflakes that are alike. Kim catches them on small pieces of dark paper so that she can see them better. Some of the snowflakes are broken because they bump into each other as they fall from the clouds.

Color.

What does Kim use to make the snowflakes look bigger?

Check.

Most snowflakes have ☐ seven ☐ six ☐ five   sides or points.

Kim looks at them on dark pieces of paper so that she can...

☐ take them to school.   ☐ make a picture.   ☐ see them better.

Write.

Why are some of the snowflakes broken?

_____

- -

_____

• Finish the snowflake.

Cassie's Ring Trick

Cassie can make a ring seem to go up and down by itself on a pencil. First, she ties a piece of thread under the eraser. Second, she ties the string to the button on her blouse. Then, she puts the ring on the pencil. When Cassie leans forward, the thread is loose, so the ring goes down. When she leans back, the ring goes up the pencil because the thread is tight.

Write.

Number the steps of Cassie's ring trick in 1, 2, 3 order.

☐   ☐   ☐

Write.

When Cassie leans forward, the ring _____.

goes up, goes down

Check.

When Cassie leans back, the ring…
☐ goes down. ☐ goes up. ☐ goes away.

Write.

Why does the ring move up the pencil?

_____

_____

•*SOMETHING EXTRA*•
Try this trick with a friend!

Old People Are Fun

Donald and Lee like to visit the home for old people. Some of their best friends live there. Old people don't climb trees or run and play tag, but they do many things that Donald and Lee like to do. They play games and tell jokes. They eat cake and ice cream. They like to listen to stories and tell them, too. Donald and Lee go there a lot because old people are fun friends to be with.

Write.

Donald and Lee like to_____
visit, watch

the home for _____ people.
young, old

Check.

Some of their best friends...

☐ play there.   ☐ live there.   ☐ go to school there.

Circle yes or no.

Old people can...

climb trees.	Yes	No
eat cake and ice cream.	Yes	No
play games and tell jokes.	Yes	No
run and play tag.	Yes	No
listen to and tell stories.	Yes	No

• SOMETHING EXTRA •

Draw a picture of yourself doing something fun with an old person.

Two Houses

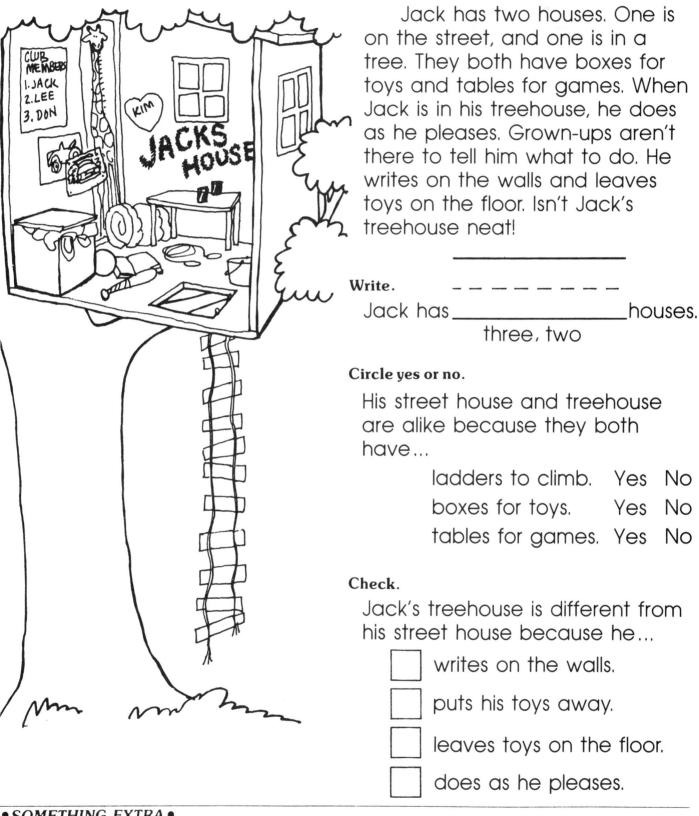

Jack has two houses. One is on the street, and one is in a tree. They both have boxes for toys and tables for games. When Jack is in his treehouse, he does as he pleases. Grown-ups aren't there to tell him what to do. He writes on the walls and leaves toys on the floor. Isn't Jack's treehouse neat!

Write.

Jack has _____ houses.
three, two

Circle yes or no.

His street house and treehouse are alike because they both have...

ladders to climb.	Yes	No
boxes for toys.	Yes	No
tables for games.	Yes	No

Check.

Jack's treehouse is different from his street house because he...

☐ writes on the walls.

☐ puts his toys away.

☐ leaves toys on the floor.

☐ does as he pleases.

•SOMETHING EXTRA•

Draw a picture of yourself climbing the ladder to Jack's treehouse.

A Better Place to Live

Lee and Maria are alike. They are both immigrants. They moved to America with their families to find a better place to live and go to school. They both learned how to speak English. Maria and Lee are different, too. Maria moved to America from Mexico, and Lee moved to America from Vietnam. Lee came in a boat, and Maria came in a plane.

Mexico

Check.

How are Lee and Maria alike?

☐ are both immigrants

☐ came from Mexico

☐ learned to speak English

☐ came to find a better place to live

☐ came in a boat

Circle.

Lee   Maria   moved to America from Vietnam.

Lee   Maria   came in a plane.

Lee   Maria   moved to America from Mexico.

Lee   Maria   came in a boat.

Vietnam

Color...

the country Maria came from red.

the country Lee came from blue.

New Dresses

Maria and Beth are wearing new dresses. Just look at their faces! Both dresses are striped with four shiny buttons. Each has a belt and a pocket for pencils. Beth's dress is blue, while Maria's is yellow. Beth's pocket is bigger with room for a kitten. Beth and Maria must shop at the very same places.

Check.

Both dresses...

☐ are striped.

☐ are yellow.

☐ have four buttons.

☐ have pockets.

☐ have belts.

Circle.

Beth's dress is   yellow / blue   with a   bigger / smaller   pocket.

Unscramble and write. _____

Maria's dress is _____ .

wlyeol

Write.

Where do Maria and Beth shop?

_____

_____

•SOMETHING EXTRA•

Color the dresses yellow and blue.

"Fetch, Dudley!"

When Donald tells Dudley to sit, Dudley rolls over. If Donald asks him to come, Dudley runs away. To surprise Dad, he tries to teach Dudley how to fetch the newspaper. Dudley rips it up! Donald will take him to dog obedience school.

Check.

What does Dudley do when Donald says, "Sit"?

- [ ] rolls over
- [ ] sits
- [ ] runs away

Circle.

"Fetch the newspaper" means ...

Circle yes or no.

Dudley will learn how to sit.	Yes	No
Dudley will learn how to fetch.	Yes	No
Dudley will learn how to read.	Yes	No
Dudley will learn to come.	Yes	No

Draw three things Dudley could learn how to fetch.

Don't Eat the Cookies!

Kim's mom bakes big cookies with gumdrops on top. Kim wants to eat one, but Mom says she must wait until after dinner. When Mom isn't looking, Kim grabs one and swallows it down. Gulp! Mom turns around and sees that one is gone. There are crumbs all over Kim's face! What does Mom say? What does Kim say?

Check.

Kim wants to eat a

☐ pie.

☐ cookie.

☐ cake.

Circle.

What does Kim do when Mom isn't looking?

bakes cookies   eats a cookie   puts gumdrops on top

Underline.

Mom knows that Kim ate a cookie because ...

all the cookies are gone.   there are crumbs on Kim's face.

Write.

What does Mom say? What does Kim say?

Wishing for Snow

Beth and Kim wish that it would snow. They want to make a snowman and throw snowballs at Jack and Lee. So they try to make it snow when Kim spends the night at Beth's house. They toss a penny in a wishing well and break a wishbone after dinner. They wish upon a falling star. They put a rabbit's foot and a four-leaf clover under their pillows for good luck. Then, Beth and Kim wish and dream of snow.

Circle.

Beth and Kim wish that it would...

rain.   snow.

Write.

What do they want to do in the snow?

_____

– –

_____

Check.

		make a wish with it	brings good luck
	wishbone	☐	☐
	rabbit's foot	☐	☐
	four-leaf clover	☐	☐
	falling star	☐	☐
	wishing well	☐	☐

• SOMETHING EXTRA •   Draw a picture of something you have wished for.

Color.

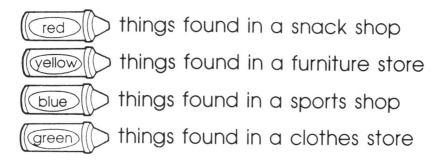

red ⟩ things found in a snack shop
yellow ⟩ things found in a furniture store
blue ⟩ things found in a sports shop
green ⟩ things found in a clothes store

♡ tent   ♡ lamp   ♡ chair   ♡ lemonade
♡ cookies   ♡ pants   ♡ skis   ♡ coat
♡ table   ♡ sofa   ♡ hot dog   ♡ dress
♡ canteen   ♡ mittens   ♡ basketball   ♡ ice cream

• Draw a blue ☐ around the words that start with the letter **C**.
• Color each **C** word you find in the stores.

Jack's Plan

Jack has a plan. He wants to take his parents out for lunch to thank them for all the nice things they have done for him. His sister Jessica will go, too, so she won't feel left out. Jack saves the money he makes from doing jobs around his house and neighborhood. He is thrifty because he saves his money. Jack has ten dollars. He needs twenty dollars to take everyone out to lunch.

Circle yes or no.

What nice things do you think Jack wants to thank his parents for?

taking him to fun places	Yes	No
making him feel left out	Yes	No
fixing good food to eat	Yes	No
helping him with his homework	Yes	No

Check.

Where do you think Jack will take his parents and Jessica?

☐ to the zoo ☐ to a restaurant ☐ to the park

Circle.

Jack needs twenty dollars. He has ten dollars. How much more does he need?

one dollar   five dollars   ten dollars

Check.

Jack is thrifty because he ...

☐ saves his money. ☐ spends his money.

The Oldest

Sometimes, Jack likes being the oldest. He can stay up one hour later, and he can go places by himself. He gets a bigger allowance for helping around the house, and he gets to spend the night at Donald's.

Sometimes, Jack doesn't like being the oldest. He has to babysit his sister and let her tag along with him and his friends. He has more jobs to do around the house and has to act more like a grown-up.

Underline.

Jack likes being the oldest   all of the time.
                                some of the time.

Circle.

Where do you think Jack can go by himself?

    to the store   to the mountains   to the park

Check.

What jobs do you think Jack has to do that Jessica doesn't have to do?

☐ dust the living room   ☐ dry the dishes   ☐ paint the house

Write. _____

_ _ _ _ _ _ _ _ _ _ _

Jessica is _____ than Jack.

                older, younger

• *SOMETHING EXTRA* •

Draw a picture of a place you can go to by yourself.

Is a Pillow a Bear?

Lee's baby sister hugs a big pillow and calls it a bear. She bangs on a pot and calls it a drum. She sits under an umbrella and calls it a tent. She builds things with books and calls them big blocks. She rides on a rake and calls it a horse. She puts a lampshade on her head and calls it a hat. Grown-ups just smile and think she is cute most of the time.

Underline.

Lee's baby sister thinks   everything is a toy.
grown-ups are cute.

Write.

What do you think Lee's baby sister would do with a basket?

_____

_ _

_____

Circle.

A big pillow makes a good bear because it is...
hard.   soft.

Check.

When do you think grown-ups **wouldn't** think she is cute?

☐ She throws a plate and calls it a spaceship.

☐ She sits in a sack and calls it a ship.

☐ She draws with Mom's lipstick and calls it a crayon.

•SOMETHING EXTRA•

Draw a picture of something you played with when you were little that wasn't really a toy.

Lee Did It!

Miss Freed asks Beth to watch the class while she goes to the office to get some paste. After she leaves the room, Lee jumps up and grabs Beth's paper. Then, he runs to the back of the room and draws a silly picture of the teacher on the back, the kind of silly picture that teachers just don't like. Beth runs back and gets her paper back. Just as she takes her paper, Miss Freed walks in the door. Miss Freed looks at the class. Everyone is working hard on the spelling lesson. She looks at Beth.

Circle.

Miss Freed probably thinks that   Beth / Lee   drew the silly picture.

Write.

How do you think Beth feels?

_____

- -

_____

Check.

Lee is probably hoping that Miss Freed thinks that...

☐ he drew the picture.   ☐ Beth drew the picture.

Underline.

What do you think Miss Freed will do?

She will have Beth stay after school.

She will talk to Beth and find out what happened.

• *SOMETHING EXTRA* •

Write about a time that you were blamed for something you didn't do.

A Good Home for Henrietta

Cassie can't keep Henrietta the kangaroo, so she will find a good home for her. She makes signs about the kangaroo and puts them around the neighborhood. A family called the Magroons calls and comes over to meet Henrietta. They like her and want to take her home. What do you think Cassie will want to know before she lets them take Henrietta?

Circle yes or no.

Cassie wants the Magroons to...

let Henrietta run around in the streets.	Yes	No
tie her to a tree and leave her there.	Yes	No
give her lots of love and attention.	Yes	No
put a collar on her with her name and address.	Yes	No
give her a nice bed to sleep in.	Yes	No
train her to be a good kangaroo.	Yes	No
take her for nice, long walks in the park.	Yes	No

Write.

Why do you think Cassie can't keep Henrietta?

_____

_____

Circle.

Would you like to give Henrietta a nice home?

Yes   No

Which Brand Is the Best?

Donald takes Dudley to the store to buy a big bag of dog food. Each dog food maker says that his dog food is the best. If Donald buys Ben-L-Train, Dudley will have a longer life. If he buys Best Ever Dog Chow, Dudley will get the extra vitamins he needs for strong bones and teeth. If Donald buys Bits and Bits, Dudley will have good health and no bad dog breath.

Match.

Best Ever Dog Chow	good health and no bad dog breath
Ben-L-Train	extra vitamins for strong bones and teeth
Bits and Bits	help Dudley live a longer life

Write.

What are the dog food makers trying to get Donald to do?

_____

- - - - - - - - - - - - - - - - - - - -

_____

Circle.

Which sack of food would you buy?

Ben-L-Train

Best Ever Dog Chow

Bits and Bits

•*SOMETHING EXTRA*•

Pretend that you are a dog food maker. Write a sentence on the bag to get Donald to buy Doggy Delight for Dudley.

Arnold Tries to Make Friends

Arnold the Bully is trying to make friends. He isn't sure what he should do because he has always been a bully. He tries to buy friends by giving away his lunch and his toys. He listens to kids and doesn't boss them around. He takes turns and doesn't call names. He brags about what his dad does at work and shows off on the bars at recess.

Circle the good ways and the bad ways to make friends.

Arnold

tries to buy friends.	Good	Bad
listens to what kids say.	Good	Bad
doesn't boss kids around.	Good	Bad
takes turns.	Good	Bad
brags about his dad.	Good	Bad
shows off on the bars.	Good	Bad

Write.

Why isn't Arnold sure about what he should do to make friends?

_____

_ _

_____

• *SOMETHING EXTRA* •

Make a list of more good ways to make friends.

Finders, Keepers

On his way home from the park, Lee finds a baseball mitt under a bush. Jack tells Lee to keep the mitt because he is the one who found it. Donald tells him to leave it there. Arnold tells Lee to take it to the Lost and Found Department at the park. Lee looks inside the mitt. He can see a name and a telephone number.

Jack   Donald   Lee   Arnold

Circle.

Jack tells Lee to keep the mitt.   Right   Wrong

Donald tells him to leave it under the bush.   Right   Wrong

Arnold tells him to take it to the Lost and Found. Right   Wrong

Underline.

Donald tells Lee to leave the mitt where he found it because...

the owner might look for it there.   the mitt belongs to him.

Write.

What do you think Lee will do?

_____

_ _

_____

The Bed Hog

Dudley has a nice dog basket with a big, blue pillow, but he never sleeps in it. He likes to sleep with Donald. He brings his toys to bed late at night when Donald is asleep. When Donald wakes up in the morning, he finds a big bed hog in his bed.

Draw and color.

- one brown shoe on the bed
- three red balls on the bed
- two blue socks on the bed
- two bones in the ☁
- one pink rabbit next to Dudley
- one rubber steak

Dudley's Dream House

Dudley wants his dog house to be different from the other dog houses on his block. He gets some paint. He gets green paint, orange paint, red paint and purple paint. He paints all morning. He paints all afternoon and doesn't stop for lunch. He invites all of his dog friends to see his new dream house. After his friends see the house, they go home and get some green paint, orange paint, red paint and purple paint.

Follow the directions to see how Dudley paints his dream house.

Color.

     1 – Purple

     2 – Orange

     3 – Red

     4 – Green

Lost at Sea

Lee's baby sister sits in Mom's basket and pretends it's a boat lost in a storm. She meets a giant sea turtle who knows the way home. She ties a rope to its tail and looks for some land. She sees a long dock with a light at the end. She shouts, "Ahoy, ahoy!" which means "hello" on a ship. The giant sea turtle takes her safely to shore and ties up the boat. Then, it goes back out to sea to find more people to help.

Follow the directions.

Draw a on Lee's sister's head.

Draw a on the boat.

Color the giant sea turtle green.

Draw and color two big .

Write what Lee's sister shouts in the ⬭.

Draw a rope from the boat to the sea turtle.

Pizza King

The Magroons take their new kangaroo to Pizza King for dinner. Henrietta orders a medium-size pizza with olives, mushrooms and pieces of bacon. She also orders two toppings just for kangaroos, big leaves and some nice green grass. Would you eat a piece of Henrietta's pizza?

Draw and color on the pizza.

- three black ⬭ olives

- five 🍄 mushrooms

- four 〰️ pieces of bacon

- two 🍃 leaves

- some nice green 🌱 grass

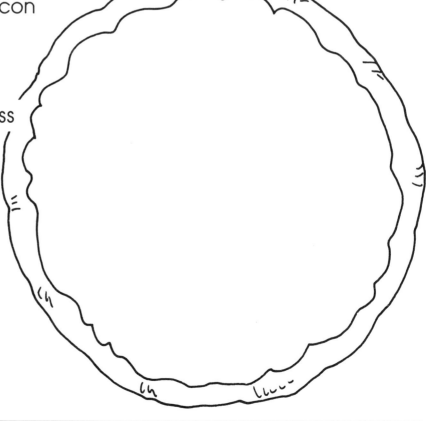

The Best Face Ever

The sun is shining, but Donald feels like it is raining inside. His pet turtle died last night, and he buried it under a tree this morning. His friends want to cheer him up. Cassie does a magic trick, but Donald doesn't smile. Jack tells his best "knock-knock" joke, but Donald doesn't smile. Maria makes her best face ever. Donald starts to smile.

Check.

When Donald feels like it is raining inside, he is ...

☐ surprised. ☐ sad.

Write.

What would you do to cheer Donald up?

_____

– –

_____

Circle.

Has one of your pets ever died?

Yes   No

Check.

His friends try to cheer him up because they ...

☐ know how he feels.

☐ didn't like his turtle.

•SOMETHING EXTRA•

Draw the best face ever to make Donald smile.

Lee Feels Left Out

Donald, Jack and Lee are climbing on the jungle gym. Jack asks Donald to come over to his house after school to play. Lee thinks Jack will ask him, too, but Jack doesn't. Lee feels left out. He goes over to the classroom door to wait for the bell. He can see Donald and Jack on the jungle gym smiling and laughing. He can see Arnold swinging by himself on the bars.

Circle.

Have you ever felt left out like Lee?

Yes   No

Write.

What do you think Lee should do now?

_____

_____

_____

Check.

Jack

could have...

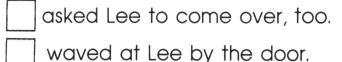

☐ asked Lee to come over, too.

☐ waved at Lee by the door.

☐ asked Donald to come over when Lee wasn't with them.

Underline.

Donald could have asked Jack if...

Arnold could come over, too.

Lee could come over, too.

Answer Key
Reading
for
Understanding
Grade 2

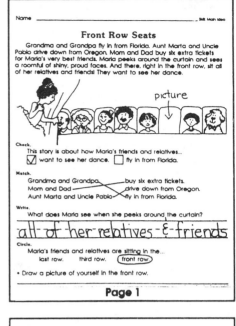

Front Row Seats

Grandma and Grandpa fly in from Florida. Aunt Marta and Uncle Pablo drive down from Oregon. Mom and Dad buy six extra tickets for Maria's very best friends. Maria peeks around the curtain and sees a roomful of shiny, proud faces. And there, right in the front row, sit all of her relatives and friends! They want to see her dance.

Check.
This story is about how Maria's friends and relatives...
☑ want to see her dance. ☐ fly in from Florida.

Match.
Grandma and Grandpa — buy six extra tickets.
Mom and Dad — drive down from Oregon.
Aunt Marta and Uncle Pablo — fly in from Florida.

Write.
What does Maria see when she peeks around the curtain?
all of her relatives & friends

Circle.
Maria's friends and relatives are sitting in the...
last row.   third row.   (front row.)

• Draw a picture of yourself in the front row.

Page 1

Marry Me, Beth!

At recess time, the kids wait for Beth by the door. They all want her to be their friend. If the girls play "Marry Me," the boys don't get mad if Beth catches them. They don't seem to run so fast. If the class plays dodgeball, Beth is the first one picked. Beth is nice to everyone, and everyone is nice to her.

Check.
This story is about a girl who ☐ wants friends.
☑ everyone likes.

Circle yes or no.
How do you know that everyone likes Beth?
Beth is the last one picked for dodgeball.   Yes (No)
Kids wait for her by the door at recess.   (Yes) No
The boys don't get mad if she catches them.   (Yes) No
She is the first one picked for dodgeball.   (Yes) No
Everyone is mean to her.   Yes (No)

Circle and color.
When Beth catches them in "Marry Me," the boys are...

Page 2

Shortcut

After the school play on a dark, dark night, the gang walks by a dark, dark lot. Jack wants to take a shortcut and asks, "Who will go in first?" No one says a word. Everyone knows that ghosts play there. Cassie says, "I'll be brave and go in first." She runs quickly through the lot. Then she yells, "Okay, Jack, now it's your turn." Jack does not want to go!

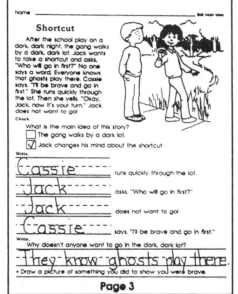

Check.
What is the main idea of this story?
☐ The gang walks by a dark lot.
☑ Jack changes his mind about the shortcut.

Write.
Cassie runs quickly through the lot.
Jack asks, "Who will go in first?"
Jack does not want to go!
Cassie says, "I'll be brave and go in first."

Write.
Why doesn't anyone want to go in the dark, dark lot?
They know ghosts play there.

• Draw a picture of something you did to show you were brave.

Page 3

If Cassie Were Invisible

If Cassie were invisible, she would go to school and not do any work because her teacher couldn't see her. She would stay up late and go to bed in her jeans and t-shirt. Then, she stops and thinks. If she were invisible, she wouldn't get any apple pie and ice cream. And no one would ask her to play if they couldn't see her. Maybe being invisible wouldn't be so much fun after all.

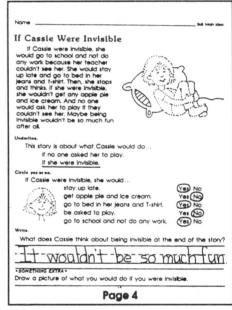

Underline.
This story is about what Cassie would do...
if no one asked her to play.
If she were invisible.

Circle yes or no.
If Cassie were invisible, she would...
stay up late.   (Yes) No
get apple pie and ice cream.   Yes (No)
go to bed in her jeans and T-shirt.   (Yes) No
be asked to play.   Yes (No)
go to school and not do any work.   (Yes) No

Write.
What does Cassie think about being invisible at the end of the story?
It wouldn't be so much fun.

• SOMETHING EXTRA •
Draw a picture of what you would do if you were invisible.

Page 4

What Does It Say?

When it's time to go home from school, Miss Freed gives Donald a note for his mom and dad. Donald wonders about what it says. Did Miss Freed see me stick out my tongue in spelling? Did she see me cut in line for a drink of water? Did she see that funny picture of the new girl and pass it around in reading? Donald says to himself, "I'll be really good tomorrow!"

Check.
What is the main idea of this story?
☑ Donald wonders what the note says.
☐ Donald cuts in line for a drink.

Circle yes or no.
Donald wonders if Miss Freed saw him...
stick his tongue out.   (Yes) No
throw his lunch away.   Yes (No)
cut in line.   (Yes) No
pass a note.   (Yes) No

Can Dudley come to school next Tuesday and cook a Chinese dinner for our class?
Thank you,
Miss Freed

Check.
Read Donald's note.
Miss Freed wants   ☑ Dudley
☐ Mom and Dad
to cook a Chinese dinner for her ☐ mother ☐ Monday.
next ☑ class ☑ Tuesday.

Page 5

Story Without Words

Tonight, Maria will dance in the story called "Sleeping Beauty." She will help tell the story without talking or singing. Dancing that tells a story without words is called "ballet." Maria has been taking ballet lessons since she was six. She has learned special ways of moving her feet in ballet that are called "positions."

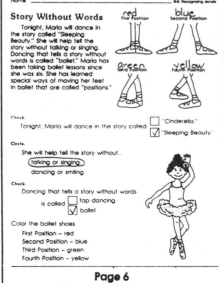

red First Position   blue Second Position
green Third Position   yellow Fourth Position

Check.
Tonight, Maria will dance in the story called ☐ "Cinderella."
☑ "Sleeping Beauty."

Circle.
She will help tell the story without...
(talking or singing)
dancing or smiling.

Check.
Dancing that tells a story without words
is called ☐ tap dancing.
☑ ballet.

Color the ballet shoes.
First Position – red
Second Position – blue
Third Position – green
Fourth Position – yellow

Page 6

Excuse Me!

Cassie and Jackie go to the movies on Saturday afternoon. They will see a movie and three cartoons for only two dollars each. Cassie stands in line to buy popcorn and soft drinks. Jackie finds two good seats for them in the second row. The lights go off, and the movie starts. Cassie is trying to find her seat. "Oops! Excuse me!" It's very hard to find your seat when it's dark at the movies on Saturday afternoon.

Write.
Where do Cassie and Jackie go on Saturday afternoon?
to the movies

Underline.
Cassie stands in line to buy candy _popcorn_ and soft drinks. milk.

Check.
Jackie finds two good seats for them in the ☐ third row.
☑ second

Write.
What does Cassie say when she can't find her seat?
"Oops! Excuse me."

Page 7

Cannonball Contest

Cassie, Kim and Beth are having a cannonball contest. You will be the judge! The girls go to the deep end of the pool. They all stand on the same line and wait until the coast is clear. Then, they run their fastest and jump high into the air. They grab their knees and put their heads down low. Splash! Which girl wins the contest?

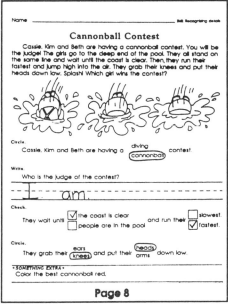

Circle.

Cassie, Kim and Beth are having a **diving** (cannonball) contest.

Write.

Who is the judge of the contest?

__I am__

Check.

They wait until ☑ the coast is clear and run their ☐ slowest.
☐ people are in the pool ☑ fastest.

Circle.

They grab their ears (knees) and put their (heads) arms down low.

• SOMETHING EXTRA •
Color the best cannonball red.

Page 8

Midnight

Kim has a horse with a spot on her nose and a long, fluffy tail. Kim calls her Midnight because of the time she was born. Her color is tan (yellow and brown). Midnight is called a filly because she's a girl and younger than four. Midnight likes to eat hay and small pieces of candy. She can run fast and jump over fences.

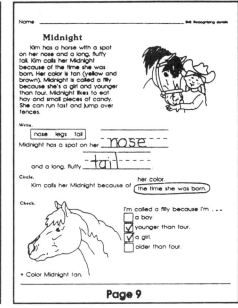

Write.

nose legs tail

Midnight has a spot on her __nose__

and a long, fluffy __tail__

Circle.

Kim calls her Midnight because of her color.
(the time she was born.)

Check.

I'm called a filly because I'm . . .
☐ a boy.
☐ younger than four.
☑ a girl.
☐ older than four.

• Color Midnight tan.

Page 9

Wanted!

Kim reads the wanted poster about One-Eyed Harry who robbed the bank last night. Harry has two mean and beady eyes. He wears a patch over one eye just to scare people. He's short, about five feet tall, and wears a polka-dot bandanna. He has a dirty beard and a long, pointed nose. He has a wart or two on the end. No one has gotten close enough to count them. He wears an earring in one ear, and he has one front tooth missing.

Draw two warts.

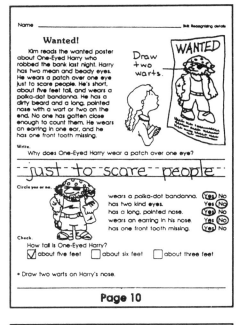

Write.

Why does One-Eyed Harry wear a patch over one eye?

__just to scare people__

Circle yes or no.

wears a polka-dot bandanna. (Yes) No
has two kind eyes. Yes (No)
has a long, pointed nose. (Yes) No
wears an earring in his nose. Yes (No)
has one front tooth missing. (Yes) No

Check.

How tall is One-Eyed Harry?
☑ about five feet ☐ about six feet ☐ about three feet

• Draw two warts on Harry's nose.

Page 10

Lemonade for Sale

Jack and Lee start a business selling lemonade. First, they make a stand from Lee's picnic table. Second, they go to the store to buy a box of lemons and a sack of sugar. Third, they squeeze the lemons and pick out the seeds. Fourth, they mix the lemon juice with sugar and cold water. Would you like to buy a cold glass of lemonade from them? It's only fifteen cents.

Circle.

Jack and Lee start a **show** (business) selling (lemonade.) hot dogs.

Write in 1, 2, 3, 4 order.

go to the store to buy lemons and sugar. [2]
make a stand from Lee's picnic table. [1]
mix the lemon juice with sugar and water. [4]
squeeze the lemons and pick out the seeds. [3]

Check.

You can buy a cold glass of lemonade for ☑ fifteen cents.
☐ ten cents.

Page 11

Don't Dally!

Beth's Mom sends her to the store to buy bread, butter and milk. On her way to the store, Beth sees a fire engine parked along the street, but she doesn't dally. Then, she sees an organ grinder. Beth keeps on walking. Next, she meets some friends who ask her to play ball. She doesn't dally and walks into the store. Now, she can't remember what to buy!

Check.

Beth's Mom sends her to the store to buy...
☐ an organ grinder. ☑ bread, butter and milk.

Write in 1, 2, 3 order.

meets some friends who ask her to play ball. [3]
sees a fire engine parked along the street. [1]
sees an organ grinder. [2]

Circle.

"Dally" means to (take too much time to do something.)
do something in a hurry.

Color.

Help Beth remember what to buy. Draw a picture of bread, butter and milk.

Page 12

Dudley Goes to School

Donald takes Dudley to a special school for dogs. Yesterday, Dudley learned how to do those usual dog things like how to sit, fetch and come. Today, he learns how to drive a car. Tomorrow, he will learn how to cook a Chinese dinner. Dudley is a very smart dog. He is at the top of his class. Do you know a dog that can drive a car or cook a Chinese dinner?

Write.

Where does Donald take Dudley?

__to a special school for dogs__

Write.

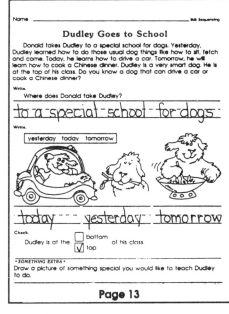

yesterday today tomorrow

__today__ __yesterday__ __tomorrow__

Check.

Dudley is at the ☐ bottom ☑ top of his class.

• SOMETHING EXTRA •
Draw a picture of something special you would like to teach Dudley to do.

Page 13

Dudley's Portrait

Donald likes to paint portraits of people and animals. He feels lucky because he can draw and paint well. First, he draws Dudley's portrait with a pencil. Second, he erases and makes the changes he wants. Third, he colors Dudley's portrait with paints. Dudley is curious to see how his portrait will look.

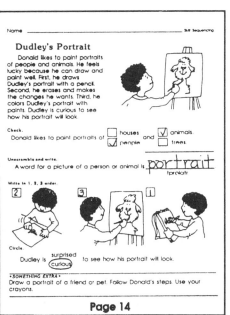

Check.

Donald likes to paint portraits of ☐ houses and ☑ animals.
☑ people ☐ trees.

Unscramble and write.

A word for a picture of a person or animal is __portrait__
tprolalt

Write in 1, 2, 3 order.

[2] [3] [1]

Circle.

Dudley is **surprised** (curious) to see how his portrait will look.

• SOMETHING EXTRA •
Draw a portrait of a friend or pet. Follow Donald's steps. Use your crayons.

Page 14

Not Now, Dudley!

Donald and Lee are playing with trucks. Dudley feels left out. He brings them his ball, wagging his tail. "Not now, Dudley," say Donald and Lee. Dudley is sad and hurt. So he gets a stick, a good one to fetch, and gives them his best sad dog look. Donald and Lee know that dogs have feelings too. "Now Dudley!" they say.

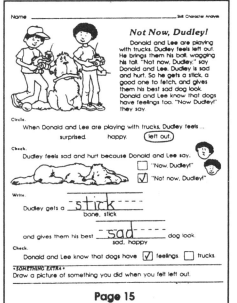

Circle.

When Donald and Lee are playing with trucks, Dudley feels ...
surprised. happy. (left out.)

Check.

Dudley feels sad and hurt because Donald and Lee say.
☐ "Now, Dudley!"
☑ "Not now, Dudley!"

Write.

Dudley gets a __stick__
bone, stick

and gives them his best __sad__ dog look.
sad, happy

Check.

Donald and Lee know that dogs have ☑ feelings. ☐ trucks.

• SOMETHING EXTRA •
Draw a picture of something you did when you felt left out.

Page 15

Company

All of Lee's relatives are coming for dinner tonight. Lee is not very happy. He'll have to be nice, like sugar and spice, and wear that suit Grandma gave him. When they pat him on the head and ask, "How is school?" he will smile and say that it's fine. He will sit on the couch and pretend not to be bored when they talk about Aunt Martha's bad back.

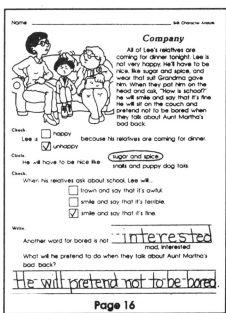

Check.

Lee is ☐ happy because his relatives are coming for dinner.
☑ unhappy

Circle.

He will have to be nice like (sugar and spice.)
snails and puppy dog tails.

Check.

When his relatives ask about school, Lee will...
☐ frown and say that it's awful.
☐ smile and say that it's terrible.
☑ smile and say that it's fine.

Write.

Another word for bored is not __interested__
mad, interested

What will he pretend to do when they talk about Aunt Martha's bad back?

__He will pretend not to be bored.__

Page 16

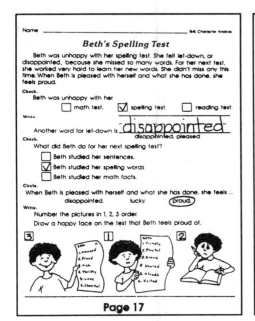

Beth's Spelling Test

Beth was unhappy with her spelling test. She felt let-down, or disappointed, because she missed so many words. For her next test, she worked very hard to learn her new words. She didn't miss any this time. When Beth is pleased with herself and what she has done, she feels proud.

Check.
Beth was unhappy with her
☐ math test. ☑ spelling test. ☐ reading test.

Write.
Another word for let-down is **disappointed**
disappointed, pleased

Check.
What did Beth do for her next spelling test?
☐ Beth studied her sentences.
☑ Beth studied her spelling words
☐ Beth studied her math facts.

Circle.
When Beth is pleased with herself and what she has done, she feels...
disappointed. lucky. (proud.)

Write.
Number the pictures in 1, 2, 3 order.
Draw a happy face on the test that Beth feels proud of.

Page 17

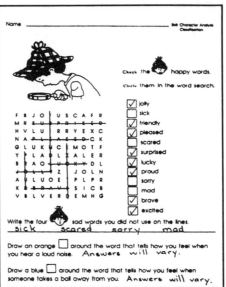

Check the 😊 happy words.
Circle them in the word search.

☑ jolly
☐ sick
☑ friendly
☑ pleased
☐ scared
☑ surprised
☑ lucky
☑ proud
☐ sorry
☐ mad
☑ brave
☑ excited

Write the four 😟 sad words you did not use on the lines.
sick   scared   sorry   mad

Draw an orange ☐ around the word that tells how you feel when you hear a loud noise. Answers will vary.

Draw a blue ☐ around the word that tells how you feel when someone takes a ball away from you. Answers will vary.

Page 18

Read and finish the sentences. Draw faces to show how Jack feels.

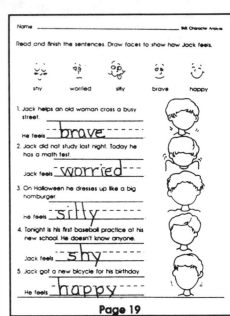

shy   worried   silly   brave   happy

1. Jack helps an old woman cross a busy street.
He feels **brave**

2. Jack did not study last night. Today he has a math test.
Jack feels **worried**

3. On Halloween he dresses up like a big hamburger.
he feels **silly**

4. Tonight is his first baseball practice at his new school. He doesn't know anyone.
Jack feels **shy**

5. Jack got a new bicycle for his birthday.
He feels **happy**

Page 19

Lacy Patterns

Kim likes to look at the lacy patterns of snowflakes with her magnifying glass. Most of them have six sides or six points. But she has never seen two snowflakes that are alike. Kim catches them on small pieces of dark paper so that she can see them better. Some of the snowflakes are broken because they bump into each other as they fall from the clouds.

Color.
What does Kim use to make the snowflakes look bigger?

Check.
Most snowflakes have ☐ seven ☑ six ☐ five sides or points.
Kim looks at them on dark pieces of paper so that she can...
☐ take them to school. ☐ make a picture. ☑ see them better.

Write.
Why are some of the snowflakes broken?
They bump into each other.

Finish the snowflake.

Page 20

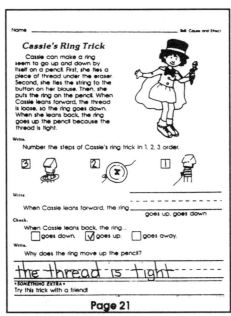

Cassie's Ring Trick

Cassie can make a ring seem to go up and down by itself on a pencil. First, she ties a piece of thread under the eraser. Second, she ties the string to the button on her blouse. Then, she puts the ring on the pencil. When Cassie leans forward, the thread is loose, so the ring goes down. When she leans back, the ring goes up the pencil because the thread is tight.

Write.
Number the steps of Cassie's ring trick in 1, 2, 3 order.

When Cassie leans forward, the ring _____
goes up, goes down

Check.
When Cassie leans back, the ring...
☐ goes down. ☑ goes up. ☐ goes away.

Write.
Why does the ring move up the pencil?
the thread is tight

• SOMETHING EXTRA •
Try this trick with a friend!

Page 21

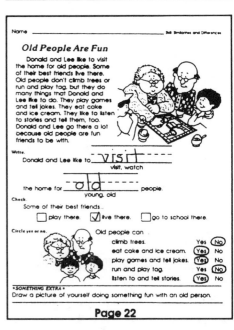

Old People Are Fun

Donald and Lee like to visit the home for old people. Some of their best friends live there. Old people don't climb trees or run and play tag, but they do many things that Donald and Lee like to do. They play games and tell jokes. They eat cake and ice cream. They like to listen to stories and tell them. Donald and Lee go there a lot because old people are fun friends to be with.

Write.
Donald and Lee like to **visit**
visit, watch

the home for **old** people.
young, old

Check.
Some of their best friends...
☐ play there. ☑ live there. ☐ go to school there.

Circle yes or no.
Old people can...
climb trees.   Yes (No)
eat cake and ice cream.   (Yes) No
play games and tell jokes. (Yes) No
run and play tag.   Yes (No)
listen to and tell stories.   (Yes) No

• SOMETHING EXTRA •
Draw a picture of yourself doing something fun with an old person.

Page 22

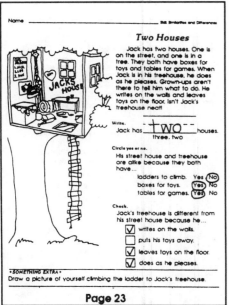

Two Houses

Jack has two houses. One is on the street, and one is in a tree. They both have boxes for toys and tables for games. When Jack is in his treehouse, he does as he pleases. Grown-ups aren't there to tell him what to do. He writes on the walls and leaves toys on the floor. Isn't Jack's treehouse neat!

Write.
Jack has **two** houses.
three, two

Circle yes or no.
His street house and treehouse are alike because they both have...
ladders to climb. Yes (No)
boxes for toys. (Yes) No
tables for games. (Yes) No

Check.
Jack's treehouse is different from his street house because he...
☑ writes on the walls.
☐ puts his toys away.
☑ leaves toys on the floor.
☑ does as he pleases.

• SOMETHING EXTRA •
Draw a picture of yourself climbing the ladder to Jack's treehouse.

Page 23

A Better Place to Live

Lee and Maria are alike. They are both immigrants. They moved to America with their families to find a better place to live and go to school. They both learned how to speak English. Maria and Lee are different, too. Maria moved to America from Mexico, and Lee moved to America from Vietnam. Lee came in a boat, and Maria came in a plane.

Check.
How are Lee and Maria alike?
☑ are both immigrants
☐ came from Mexico
☑ learned to speak English
☑ came to find a better place to live
☐ came in a boat

Circle.
(Lee) Maria   moved to America from Vietnam.
Lee (Maria)   came in a plane.
(Lee) Maria   moved to America from Mexico.
Lee (Maria)   came in a boat.

Color.
the country Maria came from red.
the country Lee came from blue.

Page 24

New Dresses

Maria and Beth are wearing new dresses. Just look at their faces! Both dresses are striped with four shiny buttons. Each has a belt and a pocket for pencils. Beth's dress is blue, while Maria's is yellow. Beth's pocket is bigger with room for a kitten. Beth and Maria must shop at the very same places.

Check.
☑ are striped.
☐ are yellow.
☑ have four buttons.
☑ have pockets.
☑ have belts.

Circle.
Beth's dress is yellow with a bigger pocket.
blue   smaller

Unscramble and write.
Maria's dress is **yellow**
wtyseol

Write.
Where do Maria and Beth shop?
at the very same places

• SOMETHING EXTRA •
Color the dresses yellow and blue

Page 25

IF5042 Reading for Understanding

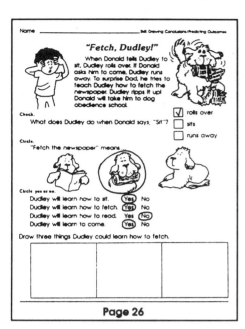

"Fetch, Dudley!"

When Donald tells Dudley to sit, Dudley rolls over. If Donald asks him to come, Dudley runs away. To surprise Dad, he tries to teach Dudley how to fetch the newspaper. Dudley rips it up! Donald will take him to dog obedience school.

Check.

What does Dudley do when Donald says, "Sit"?

- [x] rolls over
- [ ] sits
- [ ] runs away

Circle.

"Fetch the newspaper" means...

Circle yes or no.

Dudley will learn how to sit. (Yes) No
Dudley will learn how to fetch. (Yes) No
Dudley will learn how to read. Yes (No)
Dudley will learn to come. (Yes) No

Draw three things Dudley could learn how to fetch.

Page 26

Don't Eat the Cookies!

Kim's mom bakes big cookies with gumdrops on top. Kim wants to eat one, but Mom says she must wait until after dinner. When Mom isn't looking, Kim grabs one and swallows it down. Gulp! Mom turns around and sees that one is gone. There are crumbs all over Kim's face! What does Mom say? What does Kim say?

Check.

Kim wants to eat a...

- [ ] pie.
- [x] cookie.
- [ ] cake.

Circle.

What does Kim do when Mom isn't looking?

bakes cookies (eats a cookie) puts gumdrops on top

Underline.

Mom knows that Kim ate a cookie because...

all the cookies are gone. (there are crumbs on Kim's face)

Write.

What does Mom say? What does Kim say?

Answers will vary.

Page 27

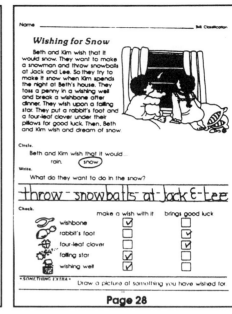

Wishing for Snow

Beth and Kim wish that it would snow. They want to make a snowman and throw snowballs at Jack and Lee. So they try to make it snow when Kim spends the night at Beth's house. They toss a penny in a wishing well and break a wishbone after dinner. They wish upon a falling star. They put a rabbit's foot and a four-leaf clover under their pillows for good luck. Then, Beth and Kim wish and dream of snow.

Circle.

Beth and Kim wish that it would...

rain. (snow)

Write.

What do they want to do in the snow?

throw snowballs at Jack & Lee

Check.

	make a wish with it	brings good luck
wishbone	[x]	[ ]
rabbit's foot	[ ]	[x]
four-leaf clover	[ ]	[x]
falling star	[x]	[ ]
wishing well	[x]	[ ]

• SOMETHING EXTRA • Draw a picture of something you have wished for.

Page 28

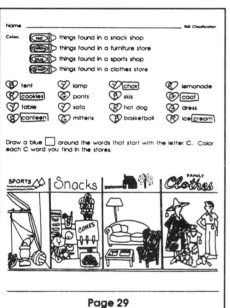

Color.

(red) things found in a snack shop
(blue) things found in a furniture store
(blue) things found in a sports shop
(green) things found in a clothes store

tent | lamp | chair | lemonade
cookies | pants | skis | coat
table | sofa | hot dog | dress
canteen | mittens | basketball | ice cream

Draw a blue ☐ around the words that start with the letter C. Color each C word you find in the stores.

SPORTS Snacks Clothes FAMILY

Page 29

Jack's Plan

Jack has a plan. He wants to take his parents out for lunch to thank them for all the nice things they have done for him. His sister Jessica will go, too, so she won't feel left out. Jack saves the money he makes from doing jobs around his house and neighborhood. He is thrifty with his money. Jack has ten dollars. He needs twenty dollars to take everyone out to lunch.

Circle yes or no.

What nice things do you think Jack wants to thank his parents for?

taking him to fun places (Yes) No
making him feel left out Yes (No)
fixing good food to eat (Yes) No
helping him with his homework (Yes) No

Check.

Where do you think Jack will take his parents and Jessica?

- [ ] to the zoo
- [x] to a restaurant
- [ ] to the park

Circle.

Jack needs twenty dollars. He has ten dollars. How much more does he need?

one dollar five dollars (ten dollars)

Check.

Jack is thrifty because he...

- [x] saves his money.
- [ ] spends his money.

Page 30

The Oldest

Sometimes, Jack likes being the oldest. He can stay up one hour later, and he can go places by himself. He gets a bigger allowance for helping around the house. And he gets to spend the night at Donald's.

Sometimes, Jack doesn't like being the oldest. He has to babysit his sister and let her tag along with him and his friends. He has more jobs to do around the house and has to act more like a grown-up.

Underline.

Jack likes being the oldest all of the time. (some of the time.)

Circle.

Where do you think Jack can go by himself?

(to the store) to the mountains (to the park)

Check.

What jobs do you think Jack has to do that Jessica doesn't have to do?

- [x] dust the living room
- [x] dry the dishes
- [ ] paint the house

Write.

Jessica is *younger* than Jack.
older, younger

• SOMETHING EXTRA •
Draw a picture of a place you can go to by yourself.

Page 31

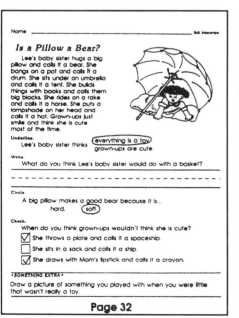

Is a Pillow a Bear?

Lee's baby sister hugs a big pillow and calls it a bear. She bangs on a pot and calls it a drum. She sits under an umbrella and calls it a tent. She builds things with books and calls them big blocks. She rides on a rake and calls it a horse. She puts a lampshade on her head and calls it a hat. Grown-ups just smile and think she is cute most of the time.

Underline.

Lee's baby sister thinks (everything is a toy.)
grown-ups are cute.

Write.

What do you think Lee's baby sister would do with a basket?

Circle.

A big pillow makes a good bear because it is...

hard. (soft)

Check.

When do you think grown-ups wouldn't think she is cute?

- [x] She throws a plate and calls it a spaceship.
- [ ] She sits in a sock and calls it a ship.
- [x] She draws with Mom's lipstick and calls it a crayon.

• SOMETHING EXTRA •
Draw a picture of something you played with when you were little that wasn't really a toy.

Page 32

Lee Did It!

Miss Freed asks Beth to watch the class while she goes to the office to get some paste. After she leaves the room, Lee jumps up and grabs Beth's paper. Then, he runs to the back of the room and draws a silly picture of the teacher on the back, the kind of silly picture that teachers just don't like. Beth runs back and gets her paper back. Just as she takes her paper, Miss Freed walks in the door. Miss Freed looks at the class. Everyone is working hard on the spelling lesson. She looks at Beth.

Circle.

Miss Freed probably thinks that (Beth) Lee drew the silly picture.

Write.

How do you think Beth feels?

Check.

Lee is probably hoping that Miss Freed thinks that...

- [ ] he drew the picture.
- [x] Beth drew the picture.

Underline.

What do you think Miss Freed will do?

She will have Beth stay after school.
She will talk to Beth and find out what happened.

• SOMETHING EXTRA •
Write about a time that you were blamed for something you didn't do.

Page 33

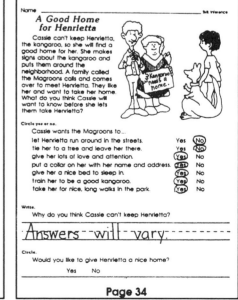

A Good Home for Henrietta

Cassie can't keep Henrietta, the kangaroo, so she will find a good home for her. She makes signs about the kangaroo and puts them around the neighborhood. A family called the Magroons calls and comes over to meet Henrietta. They like her and want to take her home. What do you think Cassie will want to know before she lets them take Henrietta?

Circle yes or no.

Cassie wants the Magroons to...

let Henrietta run around in the streets. Yes (No)
tie her to a tree and leave her there. Yes (No)
give her lots of love and attention. (Yes) No
put a collar on her with her name and address. (Yes) No
give her a nice bed to sleep in. (Yes) No
train her to be a good kangaroo. (Yes) No
take her for nice, long walks in the park. (Yes) No

Write.

Why do you think Cassie can't keep Henrietta?

Answers will vary.

Circle.

Would you like to give Henrietta a nice home?

Yes No

Page 34

Name _____

Which Brand Is the Best?

Donald takes Dudley to the store to buy a big bag of dog food. Each dog food maker says that his dog food is the best. If Donald buys Ben-L-Train, Dudley will have a longer life. If he buys Best Ever Dog Chow, Dudley will get the extra vitamins he needs for strong bones and teeth. If Donald buys Bits and Bits, Dudley will have good health and no bad dog breath.

Match.

Best Ever Dog Chow — good health and no bad dog breath
Ben-L-Train — extra vitamins for strong bones and teeth
Bits and Bits — help Dudley live a longer life

Write.

What are the dog food makers trying to get Donald to do?

buy their dog food

Circle.

Which sack of food would you buy?
Ben-L-Train
Best Ever Dog Chow
Bits and Bits

• SOMETHING EXTRA •

Pretend that you are a dog food maker. Write a sentence on the bag to get Donald to buy Doggy Delight for Dudley.

Page 35

Arnold Tries to Make Friends

Arnold the Bully is trying to make friends. He isn't sure what he should do because he's always been a bully. He tries to buy friends by giving away his lunch and his toys. He listens to kids and doesn't boss them around. He takes turns and doesn't call names. He brags about what his dad does at work and shows off on the bars at recess.

Circle the good ways and the bad ways to make friends.

	Good	Bad
tries to buy friends.		(Bad)
listens to what kids say.	(Good)	
doesn't boss kids around.	(Good)	
takes turns.	(Good)	
brags about his dad.		(Bad)
shows off on the bars.		(Bad)

Write.

Why isn't Arnold sure about what he should do to make friends?

He's always been a bully.

• SOMETHING EXTRA •

Make a list of more good ways to make friends.

Page 36

Finders, Keepers

On his way home from the park, Lee finds a baseball mitt under a bush. Jack tells Lee to keep the mitt because he is the one who found it. Donald tells him to leave it there. Arnold tells Lee to take it to the Lost and Found Department at the park. Lee looks inside the mitt. He can see a name and a telephone number.

Jack   Donald   Lee   Arnold

Circle.

Jack tells Lee to keep the mitt.   Right   (Wrong)
Donald tells him to leave it under the bush.   (Right)   Wrong
Arnold tells him to take it to the Lost and Found.   (Right)   Wrong

Underline.

Donald tells Lee to leave the mitt where he found it because...
(The owner might look for it there.)   the mitt belongs to him.

Write.

What do you think Lee will do?

_____
_____

Page 37

The Bed Hog

Dudley has a nice dog basket with a big, blue pillow, but he never sleeps in it. He likes to sleep with Donald. He brings his toys to bed late at night when Donald is asleep. When Donald wakes up in the morning, he finds a big bed hog in his bed.

Draw and color.

• one brown shoe on the bed
• three red balls on the bed
• two blue socks on the bed
• two bones in the
• one pink rabbit next to Dudley
• one rubber steak

Page 38

Dudley's Dream House

Dudley wants his dog house to be different from the others on his block. He gets some paint. He gets green paint, orange paint, red paint and purple paint. He paints all morning. He paints all afternoon and doesn't stop for lunch. He invites all of his dog friends to see his new dream house. After his friends see the house, they go home and get some green paint, orange paint, red paint and purple paint.

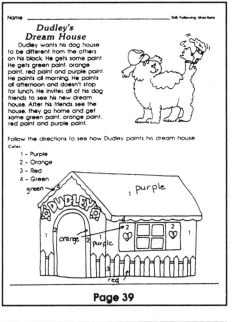

Follow the directions to see how Dudley paints his dream house.

Color.

1 – Purple
2 – Orange
3 – Red
4 – Green

Page 39

Lost at Sea

Lee's baby sister sits in Mom's basket and pretends it's a boat lost in a storm. She meets a giant sea turtle who knows the way home. She ties a rope to its tail and looks for some land. She sees a long dock with a light at the end. She shouts, "Ahoy, ahoy!" which means "hello" on a ship. The giant sea turtle takes her safely to shore and ties up the boat. Then, it goes back out to sea to find more people to help.

Follow the directions.

Draw a ▱ on Lee's sister's head.

Draw a △ on the boat.

Color the giant sea turtle green.

Draw and color two big ✿✿

Write what Lee's sister shouts in the ⬭.

Draw a rope from the boat to the sea turtle.

"Ahoy, ahoy!"

Page 40

Pizza King

The Magroons take their new kangaroo to Pizza King for dinner. Henrietta orders a medium-size pizza with olives, mushrooms and round pieces of bacon. She also orders two toppings just for kangaroos, big leaves and some nice green grass. Would you eat a piece of Henrietta's pizza?

Draw and color on the pizza.

• three black 🫒 olives
• five 🍄 mushrooms
• four 〰 pieces of bacon
• two 🍂 leaves
• some nice green grass

Page 41

The Best Face Ever

The sun is shining, but Donald feels like it is raining inside. His pet turtle died last night, and he buried it under a tree this morning. His friends want to cheer him up. Cassie does a magic trick, but Donald doesn't smile. Jack tells his best "knock-knock" joke, but Donald doesn't smile. Maria makes her best face ever. Donald starts to smile.

Check.

When Donald feels like it is raining inside, he is ...
☐ surprised.   ☑ sad.

Write.

What would you do to cheer Donald up?

Answers will vary.

Circle.

Has one of your pets ever died?
Yes   No

Check.

His friends try to cheer him up because they ...
☑ know how he feels.
☐ didn't like his turtle.

• SOMETHING EXTRA •

Draw the best face ever to make Donald smile.

Page 42

Lee Feels Left Out

Donald, Jack and Lee are climbing on the jungle gym. Jack asks Donald to come over to his house after school to play. Lee thinks Jack will ask him, too, but Jack doesn't. Lee feels left out. He goes over to the classroom door to wait for the bell. He can see Donald and Jack on the jungle gym smiling and laughing. He can see Arnold swinging by himself on the bars.

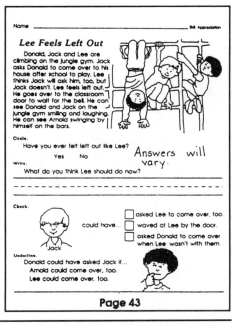

Circle.

Have you ever felt left out like Lee?
Yes   No

Write.

What do you think Lee should do?

Answers will vary.

_____

Check.

Jack could have...
☐ asked Lee to come over, too.
☐ waved at Lee by the door.
☐ asked Donald to come over when Lee wasn't with them.

Underline.

Donald could have asked Jack if...
Arnold could come over, too.
Lee could come over, too.

Page 43

                   IF5042 Reading for Understanding